Advocates, Allies, War Wounds and Battle Cries

Rebecca Laura

BookLeaf
Publishing

India | USA | UK

Presentation by *BookLeaf Publishing*

Web: www.bookleafpub.com

E-mail: info@bookleafpub.com

ISBN: 9789358317411

First edition 2023

DEDICATION

For my circle, my tribe who are my salvation.
In particular to those who have inspired the
pieces in here, my wonderful Kings among men
including my father, my grandfathers, Andrew,
Joe, Aurelien, Paul, Zander, Dennis, Ibrahim
and Tremel. My warrior women including my
mother, my sister Amy, Shanny, Emma, Lizzie,
my Lorna's, my Lucy's, Tyne, Helen, Tor,
Victoria and Zoe. And to my nieces and
nephews Yazmyn, Mayzi, Matthew, Megan and
Harri and all the other wonderful children I
know and love whose presence on this Earth
forever encourage me to be and do better every
day.

Gentle Man

Waits til late to hear the gate
An uneasiness in the air
Takes such care
To be greeted with a glare
So long since it began; bells, cries, highs, why's
But such a gentle man
Lacking in judgement or disdain
Understands there's nothing to gain
Treats all fairly, sincerely and true
Made a weary wanderer feel at home
A gentle man through and through

Gazes at the limb no longer there
People stare, unaware, that he was not to blame
The one to blame was not named
Left disintegrated, best laid fallen plans
But still a gentle man
Broken, fragmented, yet free
Lost so much time to suffering
Many hours spent recovering
Violence, a pain which can't be named
But a gentle man reclaimed

The most lost of souls
A hole left by a mother and a brother

Confronts the snow, rain, sun, sea, waves
At the mirror and feels brave
Ever the gentle man
A slice was taken from him
Misfortune favours the courageous
Gone, but her light is contagious
He shines; because of her, he can
For he is a gentle man

Forms a bridge to the other side
Losing his way, he goes wild
Searching for you in a place uninhabited
Found in the arms of another man
Ah yes, he is a gentle man
Sacrifices for his many vices
Always wanting more and more
Yet he is loyal to the core
Reassures, cures and allures
And is still a gentle man

A small boy prays for his mother's scent
Lion hearted, afraid but kind
Loves the rain, is confined to pain
From the ashes of sin from his own clan
Arises a gentle man
Powerful, brave and strong
All a 'man' should be
Yet longing for belonging
When he's already home

A gentle man is he

Royal blood with the fragility of a king
Proud to serve and take under his wing
Held a paupers knife that could take a life
Checkmate my brother, I win and I can,
Snatch victory from the jaws of defeat
And be simply a gentle man

Colours To The Mast

I'm a vessel that's all at sea
You'll bring serenity to the waves and to me

My fading colours are nailed to the mast
You'll fill them in neatly and fast

My cards are on the table but scatter in the
violence
You'll arrange them back in silence

I'll jump out and swim against the tide
You'll dive deep into the uninviting ocean and
drag me inside

I light a candle to combat the dark but it's
burning at both ends
You'll scorch your fingers to save mine, your
arm extends

I decide to eat but there's too much on my plate
You'll bite off more than you can chew so I
don't have to

You think I have power but you carry all mine
with you

You think I have strength but I lent it all to you
and I want you to keep it
You think I have courage but I'm afraid of the
dark pit
You think I'm different, but I'm the same as
others, they just don't show their colours

But mine are firmly tied to the mast with your
neat crayoning
And my cards are on the table the way you
rearranged them
And my candle burns as it should because you
took the pain
And my plate is perfectly balanced because you
consumed some on my behalf

And you're the one with the power and the
strength and the courage and the difference
And the beauty and light with which I am
honoured to be in the shadow of
And yours is the soul that saves mine by simply
being in the same space, holding it, intimately
and tenderly, in a way I did not know I needed

And you save me
And I hope that in some space, time or place,
that I save you

Small Things

You were caught out before
Drove you to cry on your bedroom floor
Drive you to the drive-thru
Self pitying but you know you're grew
But you're my ally
Those rules that you abide by or defy
Scream your battle cry and magnify

All those small things
You need your big wins
Mama brings all the kings with her flings
And you're ashamed and afraid
That maybe she's lost her way, but it's ok
It's just the small things

Your brother has your heart and soul
Flying off the handle, it's just damage control
I fly you away on a plane
Whilst you figure out who's to blame
Cos you're my ally
And you sigh, waiting to just get by
Howl your battle cry and justify

All those small things
You need your big wins

Mama brings all the kings with her flings
And you're ashamed and afraid
That maybe she's lost her way, but it's ok
It's just the small things

Your aunt adores, cherishes you
You got her temper
Wear your heart on your sleeve too
I get you a ticket to a West End show
Alleviates the cold, makes you glow
And you're my ally
Reach the sky, keep your eyes dry
Shout your battle cry and amplify

All the small things

Joy

Sourdough bread
Baking a birthday cake
A child's smile
Your smile
The greeting of a dog
The comfort of the radio commentary
The split second of silence before a goal
A bath on a winters day
A bath on any day
Goose feather pillows
The sound of a furious ocean
A child's smiling eyes
Your smiling eyes
The rain
The mist on the heath
The sun set over London
Flowers
My mother's protective hand on my back
Your protective hand on my back
Dancing
Singing with everything
Clean sheets
A new dress
An old jumper
Wellington boots

Jumping in the river with friends
Watching children play
Indentations when you lie somewhere too long
Post-it notes
A message from my family
A message from you
The leaves in Autumn
A cold, crisp day
Walking in the hills
Time with your tribe
Time with you
My flat
My nephews tiny hand
A good new lipstick
A meaningful conversation
A meaningful conversation with you
The plane
Other cultures
Vibrant colours
Teal
Holding the door for someone
The shape of a heart
The smell of a baby
My favourite perfume
Bed time
Up time
Salmon
Hoping
Hoping with you

Love
Loving you

Fine

Things are fine. Just fine.
I need to be remind
(Did) my traits evoke hate?
My light, my joy, my heart
Noticed too late
Or not at all
But I'm fine. Just fine.
And I have light in abundance
And fear, and weakness
And a tentative, raw soul
Wear your heart on your dirty sleeve
Please
With pride
Don't hide
The world needs all of your sides
No lies
Truth, honesty and good vibes
Bad vibes
No surprise
Is that a surprise?
No one needs to be unkind
Or tear down your intentions
And mention
Your flaws
Chide and chastise

If you don't fit into ideals
And you reveal
Too much
It's beautiful
And true
And all of you

War Zone

The tree is deep rooted
Yet the earth trembles
And the wingspan is extensive
But at times is grounded
The flames are searing
Yet fail to ignite
And the branches are divided
But twist in the night

The ground is resistant
Yet shakes like a quake
And the tungsten is powerful
But shatters under impact
The waves are composed
Yet rough in the storm
And the sun beams intensely
But melts when too warm

The mind is sharp
Yet the heart wants to fight
And the hands are soft
But the fingers are worked to the bone
The home is sacred
Yet the house is abandoned
And the rain means dancing
But drowns in the silence

Harmony

Harmony was born to chaos
To the most beautiful of women
And humble of men
She was not gifted the hours most are
Or the chance to give love
But she was held and won't be let go
And she was loved and will always be

Harmony was born to song
To the sound of voices she couldn't hear
And faces she couldn't see
She wasn't gifted the minutes most are
Or the chance to find her passion
But she was held and won't be let go
And she was loved and will always be

Harmony was born to tears
To a wealth of human kindness
And people who cared and were gentle
She wasn't gifted the seconds most are
Or the chance to see the world
But she was held and won't be let go
And she was loved and will always be

Her mummy loves her

Her daddy loves her
Her sister loves her
I love her
As the universe does

Here But Gone

Here but gone
Gone but here
Unknown voice speaking unknown words
To an unknown woman
In an unknown town to an unknown number
And he'll wonder
Who will look after him
Befriend him
Find him if he's lost
And at what cost
He wouldn't want to burden
Or leave people hurting
Reverting to a child
From an adult
Not pain free
Not free
No choice on when to leave
Til then
Just breathe

Wounds

The cuts had almost vanished
I had spent many days cleaning them
Most of the time it hurt to do it
They were not symmetrical or glamorous
But had faded, almost disappeared

You looked at my skin for hours
Maybe days or weeks
You saw them
You tended to them with a delicate hand
Gently cleaning and stitching them

You had your own scars
Long since anyone touched them
You flinched when I did
Moved my hand away
Then put it back
Moved my hand away
Then put it back

You didn't like my wounds anymore
You took a shard of glass
But I didn't see you do it
You held it tightly so it cut into you first

Then you retraced your steps
You didn't like my untouched skin either
And you dug the glass right in
Ripped the stitches that you put there
And then you did it again

Fresh blood was trickling everywhere
I could feel it on my back
I had never even seen that one
It was hot, burning, scorching
And you stood there unmoved

I'll have to start again
It may hurt with more intensity
Because they're both new and old
But I'll start
And I'll finish
Again
And again if I must
And again if I must

Advocate

I find black is bold and strong
But is allowed to be scared
I find Black is fierce and headstrong
But is allowed to be wrong
I find Black is radiant and exuberant
But is allowed to be sad
I find Black to be Kings and Queens
But is allowed to be green
With jealousy or spite
Or pain or fright
And downgrade to a Knight
For a night
Or a day
Or a week
Or a year
But will rise like Maya
And aim higher
Beyond the glass ceiling
Feeling, revealing and allowing for healing
I find Black is great
And to which I can relate
And will forever advocate
Only love

Anchor

Whatever anchors you, protect it
I am anchored by the breeze and the trees
The leaves and streams
I am anchored by my tribe of warrior kings and
queens
And all their hopes and dreams
I am anchored by the children I admire
Who I inspire to aim higher
And the little ones who look up
In hope and wonderment
I am anchored by my home
And it's idiosyncrasies and imperfections
The same I see in my reflection
And in my circle,
Who encircle and protect me
I am anchored by walking and running
By writing and dancing
By listening and talking
By the sound of laughter
By Sunday night calls
I protect what anchors me
And what anchors me, protects my fall

Tones

I asked a beautiful strong girl
'Are you proud to be black?'
Of your skin, of your melanin, of your kin
Ships, hard ships, of your lips, your hips
'Yes of course' came the cry
No force, to endorse, and of course she's right
Then I was asked, 'are you proud to be white?'
I'm 47.4 per cent English
And 45.1 per cent Welsh
There's a bit left over there that belongs to the
German's
Not white ish, like super light
Like when they advertise a gaming mouse
Super light, in white
Or boxing, that weight category: super light
Or a super light motorbike
Am I proud to be white?
I'm proud to be Yorkshire
Proud to be ginger
Proud to be Welsh
Proud to be an ally
Proud for the opportunity
To praise, commend and advocate
The black community
Not easy to infiltrate, to penetrate

And neither should it be
As I work to take accountability
So beautiful black girl
I see your warrior queen blueprint
Steeped in the history of your ancestors
Held in by your steep walls
And I see your iron armour
Steeped in the history of your sufferings
But I see your smile, and hear your laughter
Steeped in the history of your joy
And I see your desire and your heart
Steeped in the history of your soul
And I'll see you're alright
I'll bare my soul as you'll bare yours
So if you'll be super black,
I'll be super white
And I'll know that it ain't anti white
It's pro black
Like if you ain't feminist, I don't want to know
you
Like if you ain't pro joy, I don't want to know
you
Like if you ain't pro black, I don't want to know
you
And I hope you can hear that loud
And if you'll be super black
I'll be super white and proud

Children of Conflict

Small child. Frail.
A little sister.
Bloody feet.
A daughter. A granddaughter.
Bloody hands.
A niece. A cousin. A friend.
Bloody head.
A wife to be. A mother to be.

Small child. Scared.
A big brother.
Shaking feet.
A son. A grandson.
Shaking hands.
A nephew. A cousin. A friend.
Shaking head.
A husband to be. A father to be.

Small child. Dead. Covered.
A brother or a sister.
Still feet.
A daughter or a son.
Still hands.
A nephew or a niece. A cousin. A friend.
Still head.

A husband or a wife.
Not to be.
A mother or a father.
Not to be.

Kin

He's little, I call him little big man
He likes dry cereal and jam sandwiches
His chubby fingers curl under onto his palm
As he shakes his hands when he gets excited
He likes the floor and getting his own way
And sometimes chips,
But he loves his sisters and brother the most
though

She's little, but not that little anymore
I still call her baby girl
She likes cuddles, when I pick her up
She wraps her legs round me really tightly still
She likes baking, and her tablet
And sometimes the TV
But she loves her sisters and brothers the most
though

He's little, but he thinks he's big now
I call him my little shnoo bear
He's 9, but he wears age 12 clothes
He likes playing games and everything in it's
place
He tells me off if I get it wrong
And sometimes he likes to help and to cook

But he loves his sisters and brother the most
though

She's little, but a little bit big now
I call her my moo
She likes hugs but pretends she doesn't
And she likes to talk but pretends she doesn't
And she likes walks and being by herself
And sometimes she likes being around others
too
But she loves her sisters and brothers the most
though

She's little, but a bit grown up now
I call her my little saviour (but not to her face)
She likes the plane and places that are not home
She likes the sea too
She likes her little job and the football
She likes it when I come home, but she would
never say that
She loves her sisters and brothers the most
though

The Best I Know

The best I know are conceived in the heart of
darkness
In the depths of distress
The most compassionate I know are birthed in
the roots of fear
In the seeds of doubt

The kindest I know have crawled grotesquely
from their fog
In the depths of abandonment
The most beautiful I know have climbed
crookedly out from their void
In the depths of emptiness

The gentlest I know have transcended from
barren space
In the depths of inadequacy
The most forgiving I know have clambered
shamefully from their worthlessness
In the depths of lonliness

Those whose hearts are the most open have
taken the hardest impact
Those whose souls are the most pure have
collided with someone else's

Those whose minds are the most thoughtful have
felt the most hurt
Those whose spirits are the most tender have
plunged the furthest

They have all stood back up taller than they ever
did before
They have all outstretched their arms longer than
they ever did before
As will you my dear friend
As will you

Collide

Collision course
Remorse
Sadness
Madness
New born
Love
In all it's forms
Gone
In haste
Without trace
Embrace
In a mess
Regress
I digress
Suppress
Sad
Mad
Had
Touch me
No, don't
Live me
Have me
No, don't
Haunt me
Go to the coast with me

Do the most with me
I do the most
Host me
Toast to me
Fate
Hate
No, not hate
Real
Raw
Raw deal
Feel
Unreal
Unravel
Travel
With me
Without me
For me
For you
Hold me
Know me
Control me
No, don't
Love me
Tell someone
Tell no one
Tell God
He knows anyway
Be afraid
Be assured

When we collide
It's makes me feel alive
When we collide
It's my favourite kind
When we collide
Nothing is left behind

What If You're Not

Surrender the notion
Erase the memory
Forget the concept
Take hold of the epilogue

Do not give up. Or let go.
As a thief to their stolen article
Or a baby's tenacious clutch
Or a predator's claws
Call upon your steely grit

You know you possess it
You're a woman
All women possess it
All women do

Eliminate the recall
Close the recollection
Slam the evocation
Reset your heart

Do not give up. Or let go.
As a thief to their loot
Or a baby's deadly grip
Or a predators hook

Call upon your resilient spirit

You know you're blessed with it
You're a woman
All women are blessed with it
All women are

No one tells you what to do if you're not.

You Missed

You missed
You aimed at me, but you missed
You grazed my arm
But you missed really
I heard you shout 'Got ya'
But you didn't
I grabbed my arm and held it tightly
You shouted something else
And shot again
I fell to the floor
I exaggerated
Like my teacher taught me at school
I flung myself down
And curled up in a ball
I could almost feel blood trickle
But I didn't
Cos you missed
You came to look at me
I decided to play dead
I wasn't really dead
Because you missed
I could feel your wide eyes staring at me
I know what your eyes look like
They look like sludge
So I imagined them in my head

You told the others I was dead
Like Narcissa Malfoy tells Voldemort
That Harry Potter is dead
She lied
Like you did
I wasn't really dead
You missed remember
Then mum shouted us for tea
So we went home
And I told her that you thought you got me
But you didn't
You missed

www.ingramcontent.com/pod-product-compliance
Lightning Source LLC
LaVergne TN
LVHW010933200726
843509LV00013B/2193